A Stroke of Luck

– Hardly!

Betty Kilgour

D1736864

DETSELIG
ENTERPRISES LTD

A Stroke of Luck: Hardly!
© 2004 Betty Kilgour

Library and Archives Canada Cataloguing in Publication

Kilgour, Betty
    A stroke of luck, hardly! / Betty Kilgour

ISBN 1-55059-275-0

    1. Kilgour,   Betty–Health.   2.   Cerebrovascular
disease–Patients–Canada–Biography. I. Title

PS8571.I492Z476 2004   362.196'81'0092   C2004-905429-5

Detselig Enterprises Ltd.
210 - 1220 Kensington Road NW
Calgary, Alberta T2N 3P5
Phone: (403) 283-0900
Fax: (403) 283-6947
Email: temeron@telusplanet.net
www.temerondetselig.com

We acknowledge the support of the Government of Canada through
the   Book   Publishing   Industry   Development   Program
(BPIDP) for our publishing program.

We also acknowledge the support of the Alberta Foundation for the
Arts for our publishing program.

ISBN 1-55059-275-0
SAN 113-0234

Cover Design: Alvin Choong
Illustrations and cover illustration: Val Lawton

A Personal Note From the Author

This is Betty Kilgour and I am writing this book to maybe help someone else who has gone through what I have. I will tell you my story. This book is not a medical text book, nor a thesis on strokes, but rather the story of my last great adventure like my other books have been. Read it and take comfort, or enjoy.

Betty

Dedication

This book is dedicated to:

Margaret Hall, my therapist at the Red Deer Hospital Stroke Program. Thank you for your expertise, professionalism and for bringing out the best in me. You helped me get my life back on track and for that I love and thank you.

And also to:

Paulo Cardano, without whom I could not live at home nor lead my new life with such meaning and joy. Paulo, thank you from the bottom of my heart. I love you.

Other Books by Betty Kilgour

The Best of Crocus Coulee

The adventures begin on her own back forty. Betty, with mud up to her knees, bread dough to her elbows and a new calf to nurse, shows that aside from a little patience, all one needs in life is a great sense of humor.

So This is Africa!

The adventurous Kilgours take their youngest daughter and their farming skills to the wilds of Africa. While Bill's herding cattle through chemical dips, Betty is entertaining, nursing and learning the ways of the locals, all the while finding humor in everything.

I'd Rather Be Shelling On Niue

In a decrepit mini (loosely termed a car), Betty zooms all over the island befriending the Islanders, learning their ways in spite of herself and inadvertently bringing home an octopus for dinner! Good thing, because Bill's cattle are disappearing.

From Dar to Zanzibar

This time, Betty joins a good friend for another trip to Africa. Poking through dukas, wandering into strangers' yards with offerings of bread and typically having a Who-Else-But-Betty-Adventure, you'll find yourself laughing over her sitcom-style life.

Sumbawanga Safari

You can try to keep Africa out of the woman, but there's no use trying to keep the woman out of Africa. Betty's on a mission to Kilangala! Full of surprises and amusing stories, our feisty traveller offers a helping hand and friendship to all who cross her path.

Crocus Coulee in Bloom

Like any typical farm wife, Betty struggles with lawn mowers that try to climb trees, hopes all the appliances don't break down the same day the house is overrun with people – which happens to be every day and reminisces about an easier time before modern conveniences.

At Home From Afar

Wherever Betty goes, she finds herself welcomed and feeling quite at home. From Crocus Coulee to Sumbawanga and from Halifax to Belfast, heartwarming hugs, handshakes and humorous stories abound for the adventurous Kilgours.

Table of Contents

Acknowledgements

There are so many people to thank and I know I will miss some. I acknowledge:

Ted Giles and and May Misfeldt for accepting this material so graciously;

Kim Robertson, my new editor. What a joy you are;

My whole family for their constant support and love;

Berend Henckel, my physiotherapist for his insightful forward;

Nick Roberts, for taking on the gigantic job of typing this material and for his support;

My Bethel Fellowship Church family for all your love, kindness and prayers;

Those who visited me and brought all types of kindness and love – you know who you are;

Our dear Dr. Reedyk and all the doctors who came to my aid;

The nurses in Calgary, Red Deer and Three Hills.

I love you all.

Foreword

I first got to know Mrs. Betty Kilgour when she was transferred from the Rehabilitation Unit in Red Deer to the acute care wing of the hospital in Three Hills. An extensive stroke had left her with limited mobility and function.

She had taken part in six months of rehabilitation with the aim to regain enough independence to return home. At that stage she wasn't able to make that transition and my first impression was that Betty would require a long-term care facility to assist her in many of the day-to-day activities.

Soon I learned that this lady had lots of willpower left in her. She was going to succeed in her goal to return home. And so she did. I got to know her as a person with determination and as a person who didn't dwell on the past. Sure she had her ups and downs, but through it all she remained positive and cheerful. With the help of her family she took back control over her life.

This is a story about adaptability. We all have obstacles to overcome in our lives. Betty cleared many of those in the period since her stroke. Not only did she clear them, but she has done it with grace and elegance.

Her story is an inspiration to all of us and she will continue to amaze us as a wife, a mother, a grandmother, a friend, a humanitarian and a writer. This book is an excellent source for people who are faced with a loss of function and provides healthcare providers with a meaningful view from the other side of the fence.

Berend Henckel, P.T.
Physiotherapist, Three Hills

One

Unplanned Adventure

I had always been very cocksure about my health. I felt nothing could happen to me. I was so able to do everything I wanted to do, I never thought about my health at all. I had a minor glitch years ago when I had a thing called an arterial arteritis which affects your eyes and I permanently lost the sight in my left eye. It is similar to a stroke but mostly affects the eyes. This was rather bothersome but I got over it in due time. I was driving, knitting, crocheting and doing everything I had always done, so I felt that was my touch with a little scare and that nothing more would happen to me. In fact I was feeling hopeful that I would be able to go ahead like my little neighbor, ninety-year-old Peggy, who has been my neighbor for fifty-four years. She is able to cut her own grass on a lawn the size of a Hutterite colony. She digs a garden a size you would not believe – she can out-dig me. And she drives a pick-up truck all over the place by herself. She even goes to town and drives the old people around. She has ducks, chickens and geese which she feeds all winter and I admire her so much, I always told my girls that when I got older, I hoped I could be just like her. But this wasn't to be.

One night – it was November 25th, I remember it very well – I had gone to bed feeling just fine, with no pain, no anything. I got up in the middle of the night and went to go to the bathroom but when my foot hit the floor I just fell down. My arms flung out like I was an exotic dancer and I shouted to Bill that I'd had a stroke. Now, how I knew I'd had a stroke, I don't have a clue. Bill got me up, put me back to bed and I was absolutely helpless. A 911 call was made and I was taken by ambulance to the Calgary Foothills Hospital where I spent a month.

At first, I just lay there completely helpless. This was odd because I had the stroke on my right side so I don't know why my left hand couldn't feed me, and my left leg – I could not walk on it. I couldn't do a thing for myself. It was very embarrassing to me. The girls had to feed me and that was strange since I'm a left-handed person but I couldn't even get my left hand up. This must have been due to the shock of the stroke. My right arm was completely paralyzed and I lost quite a bit of sight in my right eye. I was a mess and not too happy. I was weak all over – the stroke just took all my strength. It was a shock to the whole body, not just to the side on which the stroke occurred.

During the first week or two, 2 therapists would come in but there was not much we could do together. They did give me bottom-lifts to do, lifting the bottom while laying in bed, which I could do. This was the *one* thing I could move! I never knew how heavy my bottom was until then. We worked like that: they would come in once a day and we would work on the derriere and on my poor right arm which would not respond. The unresponsiveness was the worst part and I wondered how I would ever be able to cope without my right arm. It was my mainstay even though I am a lefty, but oh my, I was glad that I was a lefty because at least I did have that working eventually!

Pretty soon I was put through a battery of tests. I was very fortunate to have these tests because a lot of people can't get in or have to wait months, but somehow or other I was getting them straight away. Every other day or so I would go down for another test where they would put microphones down into my heart and they took oh-so-many tests that I can't even think of them all.

There is a little vein in my temple which had played a part in my first stroke (the arteritis) and the specialists were interested in it, so they did a biopsy and snippered a piece out. They froze my temple first so all I heard was the snip and then the necessary stitching to close the wound, but the doctor assured me the stitches matched my hair color! I asked what the biopsy looked like and he said it looked like a piece of spaghetti. As it turned out, it didn't cause this stroke. Every single test proved to be normal. I was in very good condition – in fact they found me in very good health all around. I don't know just what all they did to me but everything, including my cholesterol, was perfect. I asked them why I had the stroke and the doctors said that you don't always know why, it just happens. Well that did not satisfy me too much, but as there was no apparent reason for it, I could therefore not blame myself and so I went on.

That month in Calgary is a blur. I do remember one thing: I was lying there half asleep, and the nurse said to one of my girls, "This is one patient who will never see her home again." I thought, *Oh my goodness!* as it was my dream to get back to my own home. That was my whole dream and purpose and I was going to do it. It got my Irish up a bit and I thought, *I'll show you!* and then I kind of forgot about her words, though I didn't think it was very smart of her to say that with me listening. Anyway, that got me going and my whole purpose while in hospital was to get back to my own home. I was going to fight for it and I did. It was a very hard month. I did these little exercises, but found I could hardly stand. I had to learn how to pivot to get onto the commode and then, exhausted, I'd get back into bed. I stayed in bed for the whole month; I never even sat in a chair. This stroke was quite a thing but I was fighting it.

After four weeks, I was moved to Red Deer to the Stroke Unit. I was in the main ward for about two months and they were very basic. I didn't get much therapy during the first few months. It was quite a time in the new ward! I learned that a stroke takes so much out of a person – the level of difficulty depending on whether it was mild or a very severe one like I had. If you are going to make it through you have to learn to deal with what has been handed to you, and while this is very difficult to do, if you're going to make it through, it is *very* necessary.

I found the best way to deal with my pain and misery was to find something humorous to focus on, and there were many humorous incidents I could laugh about. Now you may ask, how could I laugh when in the throes of a stroke, but you can if you want to. If you are going to get through all the changes in your life, you'd better learn to laugh at everything a day brings as well as learn to laugh at yourself. I would look to anyone: nurses, room companions or whomever, and I would find humor in them.

I remember one old lady who was in our ward. She was a funny one and I had a lot of laughs out of her! For one thing, she was always needing the bathroom and needing a bowel movement which would not come. It was funny as she would talk to me about it so seriously, as though she was some soap opera character.

"I am going now Betty," and she would go off to the bathroom. She'd shout out "It was only gas!" I would reply "Don't worry, it will come later." And then when she did have a bowel movement, she would shout out her success. And I would say "Good for you."

I would get laughs out of things like that. You may not think it funny, but it was to me – it had to be to keep me going. She was also a little cranky. She was always phoning her husband to do or bring things. The patient man would come in with whatever the latest list required. One time, she asked him to bring her Lypsol and so he came in with a little bag with everything she had called for and she got out what she thought was Lypsol but was in fact a glue stick. I thought afterward, maybe he was passing on a little bit of a hint. I got a great laugh out of that though she didn't actually put the glue on her lips!

There was another little lady; she was a new one. I came into the room, she looked at me and asked in a very broad English manner, "Are we going to the dance tonight?"

I laughed and said "Not that I know of."

She was having a hard time, always angry with her son. He would come in faithfully every day and make her a cup of real English tea. She would give him the Dickens for spending her money. I don't know if he was or not, but they would have arguments galore about her money, that he was spending it all. He told me he was spending it on her and I'd say "Oh, I didn't know," and "Oh, is that right?"

Another patient I shared a room with was a lovely little English lady by the name of Doris, a First World War bride. Every day she'd put on a fresh silk nighty, some I'm sure came over from England: the lace all faded gold. But she'd sit there like a little queen. She also loved to knit. She had it all cast on but she never made a stitch. She'd just sit there holding the needles, smiling beatifically. I asked her what she was knitting and she said in her lovely English accent, "I'm knitting a sweater for Joe." By the amount of stitches on her needles, I figured Joe must be her little grandchild. As days passed by, she sat there holding her needles quietly. Then one day she was all excited – Joe was coming in. I couldn't wait 'til he arrived. Soon Joe came through the door: Joe was a six-foot giant and 60-years-old if he was a day!

"Hello son!" she said. "I'm going to finish your sweater soon." Doris was moved soon after to a home in Northern Alberta. I missed her.

I was always hunting for things like that to laugh about because I found I could be down in the dumps many times wondering what my future was. What would I do? Here I was so paralyzed, where was I going to go? I thought I would end up in an extended care somewhere and I kept thinking, "Is there anything I can do to get out of that?" In between the bouts of self-pity I would try to pull myself up and look for the good things. I would do my bit of therapy every day and I would have tremendous support from my family. Tremendous support! I also had support from my church family. They came consistently to see me, so I was getting on just fine, as they would get me up spiritually.

The nurses got me up physically. I would try walking which I could not do very well at all. Leaning on them I could pivot and learn other things like that. I think, in all, I was there for two months, working away and enjoying my variety of roommates and guests.

Another amusing happening at the hospital, was when my black African friends would come to visit. Usually there were a few at a time. One couple used to bring their cute little girls, all dressed up in beautiful dresses, with all sorts of ribbons in their hair. They were just so dear. With their little rosebud mouths and shining black eyes, you could not help but just love them. When they visited me, all the nurses would pop in to have a look and to listen to the chatter which could become a little loud. Also, when my friend Walter arrived – he collects people of different races as some people collect spoons – his visits were always accompanied by a visitor from another nation. At these times, I would be quizzed as to who my visitors were, why were they in Canada, how did I meet them? When my Hutterite friends arrived, there was always a stir. "How did you get to know them Betty?" I was always asked. I'd then tell them the story of how we met years before. It started out with selling vegetables, but grew to taking gifts out to them whenever I could, sharing my love of perfume with them with samples I'd give them. They stopped by the house as often as any of our other assorted visitors.

One time the nurses came running in to see me and asked if they could borrow my Polygrip, as there was a man there whose teeth wouldn't stay in. I lent it to them and thought, "Next time, they'll be asking for my teeth!" but it was fun. I enjoyed it all in a funny way.

Even with all the excitement, it could get boring though too, because I was in the wards for all those months, lying in bed. I would lie there and think and think, which is not a good thing because I would always think about how I was going to get on and worry about what was in my future. I would get very down, but I would then try to pick myself up, determined to stay positive.

The nurses were wonderful. If they saw I was down they would pull me up and it was very helpful when they would come in and tell me a story or I would tell them a story and we would get going, and I could forget my troubles for a time. I couldn't help but have these down mood swings because you're lying there and your body is gone. So much is taken from you. So many of the things I used to love to do were taken away: I used to love to drive, to take the car to town whenever I wanted. I could no longer crochet. I used to write and that was taken from me as I could not use the computer again. I used to drive all over the country to speak to school children, and that was taken. When I looked at the whole picture, it wasn't pretty. So I decided I had to look at something positive.

When I arrived in Red Deer, a doctor was assigned to me and he said I should look for a local doctor as he was too busy and could not take me on. He was a specialist and was absolutely brilliant but very hard to talk to. I never did get a real visit with him, but one day he told me he had been to Africa. Of course with me having been in Africa I could talk forever. I'm used to doctors who are chatty and have a good bedside manner and pat you on your head and this sort of thing, but this fellow was just not that way, even with Africa to bond us. However, we did get along pretty well and one day he said that he thought it was time I had a wheelchair in my room. Well, I hadn't thought about getting a wheelchair, but in a day or two, one arrived. Before this I had been in bed, even exercising in bed except when they got me out to practice walking or pivoting. This pivoting was something else, and it is something I should explain a little better.

The pivoting, as I've mentioned, was to get on to the commode as I could not walk to the bathroom. The nurses would bring it in and they would do a two-step with me. You had to be good at that and they would always be after me to practice. I was getting a little stronger by then. My strength was coming back bit by bit and so my pivoting was going quite well. And when I got my wheelchair, at least I was able then to sit up. Sitting in a wheelchair all day was not easy either and I would get tired. But it was a big and welcome change from lying in bed all day.

Two

Facing the Fear

I was on the general ward for several months and then one day, the doctor came to me and said that he wanted to put my name down for a stroke program in the hospital. (The official title of the program is the "Progressive Short Stay Rehabilitation Program, for Stroke Clients and Families and/or Caregivers" (more details are given in Appendix A.). It was a short stay rehabilitation program for stroke patients and the only way to get in was to have my name submitted by a doctor and then if accepted, I would be sent to join it.

This kind of excited me because I was getting stronger and I wanted to work as hard as I could so I could go home. That was my ultimate goal: to get back home and be with Bill. This program sounded wonderful to me. It was a progressive program, working you very hard for a few months. If they thought I could benefit from it, then I would be selected. So we signed the papers and the long wait then began to see if I was going to be accepted.

One day, the nurses came in to say that I had made it into the program. I asked, "What did I do to be accepted?" since I did not know exactly what it was and they said "Well they accept people who they think would work hard at it and not waste their time and they think you'll work hard." So the wait for *that* began until there was a space. There were four patients in the program and when one left, I would be next. I continued to practice my exercises in bed as much as I could and they took me down to the general stroke program, to the gyms and things, and I practiced there beforehand so that I would be ready for the more intense program.

Now, I was very curious about this project and I found out it was a very stiff program which was fine. I like a challenge.

I also heard it was run by an English lady who ran it like an army boot-camp! She was like the Sergeant Major. I thought all of this sounded very interesting and that I would be able to handle it. I heard more about this lady, whose name was Margaret, and I was anxious to meet her.

One day she popped in to see me. She was charming and didn't show any Army Sergeant Major traits to me! She told me that as soon as someone left the program, I would be going down to join it. There would be a room for me, but she didn't know when that would be available. And so I kept on going, working away in my room and life went on as always. When my daughters came to visit, they would take me out in the wheelchair and that was always very nice as my mind was dwelling on the program and what was ahead of me. They helped to keep my mind free.

I think one big worry for me at the time was the possibility of having another stroke. No doctor could answer that concern. No one could say, but I was on medicine to hopefully stop that from happening. I didn't want to think of it too much.

Meanwhile Bill was preparing our home for me as he was sure I was going to be returning. He took up all the carpeting and laid wooden flooring so my wheelchair would not get caught in it and also so I wouldn't trip and he had a lift put in at the back for me which was wonderful. There were even plans to put up bars for me in the bathroom and other places so that I would have help when I got home. So everyone thought I was coming home, but *I* was not so sure. I was prepared though – prepared to fight like the Dickens to get home!

Fighting to get home also meant accepting things I hadn't had to worry about before. I learned very quickly that in the hospital when you're there for any length of time, you lose all sense of dignity and decorum. You have no privacy. You can't let it bother you, and have to just get used to it. Using the commode, you have to pretend that it's just an everyday occurrence.

Another annoyance that took getting used to about the stroke was that in bed at night, I would need help moving. I would be lying in bed and they would have to come in to arrange me so that I could sleep. So they would roll me onto my side and put my legs in a certain direction. I could not do this myself and often during the night I would have moved around and I would have to call them to arrange me again.

My stroke was caused by an artery in my brain having a blockage. Of course, the big question for me was how quickly can the brain heal? But no doctor had an answer for that. They did tell me that the brain will gradually compensate sometimes for what you have lost. So sometimes, in a paralyzed arm or leg, some movement could return and so I had high hopes of that. It sounded good to me!

Three

Step by Step

After many long weeks, or so it seemed, a girl came in with the great news that I would be moving to the stroke program immediately. I was very thankful. I thought it was wonderful but I was a little scared since it would be a tough program, but I wanted so much to get strong. In a day or two, I was taken down to the ward where I had a room to myself, which was lovely.

They brought in the program as to what I was going to be doing. Every morning around 8:00 or 9:00 a.m., I was to take occupational therapy where they would mainly work on my arm and teach me to help myself get dressed. The arm was very important and they worked on that continually. I also worked on it in bed for about an hour each day. At 10:00 a.m., I usually went down for speech therapy. Although my speech was not too bad, my face had fallen down a bit on the right side and they wanted to lift it. It was strange at first – the lady would put ice in a towel and run it up and down on the right side of my face. When it was good and cold, and half frozen, she would have me smile, and smile, and smile and she would pull up the corner of my mouth. She had a mirror in front of me, and we would have a good laugh, because to me, it looked like a horse leaning over a fence chewing on a brush or something. But we did it every day, with just weekends off.

At 3:00 p.m., one hour of physiotherapy would be done with Margaret, who was in charge of my overall program. This was the big one, the tough one. This was the one where I really, *really* worked but I was so pleased to be chosen for this particular program and I thought I was very lucky. I knew it was going to be tough because I had already been told that. I had always been rather athletic and loved a challenge, and I would put my athletic abilities to work on this for sure. It was though, probably going to be the greatest challenge I had ever faced, but I was going to make it because I thought this was the one way I would get well enough to get home. Every day I would be ready for whatever activity was planned for me.

I was wheeled to all my activities because I just was not able to wheel myself. There was one lady who wheel each of us in the program to our therapy sessions. There were half a dozen of us, but she made sure we all got to our programs. When I was finished, I would be wheeled back to my room. There wasn't much time for other activities during the week.

The morning was spent working on my arm because it was completely paralyzed, and we would work on it and work on it. Afterward would come my speech therapy. As I have already said, the speech therapist would put ice in a cloth and put it to the right side of my face and I would have to sit in front of a mirror and practice smiling to bring that corner of my mouth up. This really worked! But another type of speech therapy included repeating words that my therapist spoke. I would sit there repeating "me, me, me, me," until I could sound it out. My voice had quite a croak in it. We would practice many different sounds over the one hour session, then I would be taken back to my room. After dinner, around three o'clock, I would be taken down to the real therapy with Margaret. As I've said, this therapy was very hard, but that was good. I came out of it feeling good, always extremely tired, but feeling better. It was the one time each day that I felt successful. I had worked my heart out, even overachieving at times and felt so satisfied. Aching all over, yes, but feeling I was fighting the blasted stroke on my turf.

At first, my physiotherapy program was just lying on a cot drawing my knees up to my chin, though I should not say "just" since it was hard work. I also had to move side to side and do other such movements. I didn't know I had so many places that could ache! And lifting my bottom up off the mat again and again wasn't easy. Just when I thought I had finished, Margaret would say "One more, Betty," and I would do it even when I didn't want to. It was hard but good. Gradually we moved to standing. I would stand straight up from a sitting position and that was quite an achievement because I had not been able to do that. I was getting stronger and stronger. Of course there would always be the "One more, Betty."

One thing I should tell you is that every day while I was in the hospital, I applied my makeup and did my hair. I had kept my hair permed nearly almost all my adult life, but I noticed in the hospital that as it got longer, it got curly. So now, I don't need to perm my hair. It is now naturally curly. I don't know what *that* is about. But when I notice it, I prayed to God saying thanks, but I would have preferred to have my right arm back in place of the curly hair! But I guess beggars can't be choosers. I also sprayed myself silly with perfume after my hair and makeup were done. Many of the nurses laughed about my daily rituals, but I had done it all my life and it made me feel better.

Meanwhile during the day between therapy sessions, there were many things that kept me amused and happy. One such one was my birthday. I knew some of my girls would be coming in and sure enough they did. So we were sitting there chatting and opening presents, when out of the blue one of them said "Lets go to the Moose restaurant, Mum." The Moose was a little restaurant within the hospital where you could go for a cup of tea. I thought, sure, and so off we went. Feeling happy and content in the moment, I didn't bother even combing my hair! Lo and behold, when we got there, all the women from my church had come up to help celebrate my birthday. All my kids, grandchildren and even my newly arrived great-grandchild, were there. After my initial surprise, I was wishing I'd done my hair, but I let it go and just had a good time. That was an exciting day for me which gave me a *great* boost. My family and the church women stood behind me, supporting me, during my entire time in hospital. They were wonderful.

I looked forward to these kinds of things in between all the exercising, which kept me busy. I actually had very little spare time with the hour-long therapies. Afterward, I would go for my meals in the dining room. At first I had my meals in my room, but then decided I needed the social part of it, so I asked to go to the dining room. Through this I got to meet a number of other people. In the program I was in, there were only four of us but there were many other people taking therapy and some were in worse straights than me. Seeing others who were not as well as I was actually did me good. Some would never leave the hospital and it made me realize I was not so badly done by at all. There were many blessings I enjoyed, such as being able to speak. Betty Kilgour not being able to speak was a terrifying thought – me, the mouth of the town! Some of these people could not even do that and so they were much worse off than I was.

There was one girl there who came in with a stroke and while she was there she fell and broke her hip. Oh, that was a real hard one. I ached for her. She was so down, we all did whatever we could to cheer here. She actually left the hospital before I did though, doing quite well. I never imagined that I was soon to have a similar problem.

One day while sitting in my wheelchair, I reached for something on the bedside table. At the time, I thought it was terribly important that I have it and I was determined to get it! I couldn't tell you now what I thought was so important. Thinking that I could reach it, I stretched and stretched until I finally pulled myself right out of the chair and fell down.

I just thought that I had bruised my dignity more than anything else because I didn't feel anything, but the next morning, when I woke up and went to get up, oh boy, did it hurt across my rib cage. I'd been told that since it was such a smooth fall, there was nothing to worry about. The pain would go away and I was probably just shaken.

I went to therapy anyway and told Margaret that I had fallen, so we took it a little easier. She put hot packs on my rib cage and for the rest of the week, we continued with the therapy. I was still having a hard time so the doctor decided to take an x-ray and sure enough – I had a cracked rib! I thought it was quite funny, because I had felt certain I'd hurt something so I was quite pleased when I discovered that, sure enough, I had made a correct diagnosis. However, they don't do anything for a cracked rib anyway. It got better gradually. My rib did hurt quite badly at times, particularly in the morning with that first get-up movement. When I went down for therapy, Margaret would help with the heat packs before we started the exercises which helped a lot. Gradually the pain eased, but I couldn't make any sudden movements for a long time after.

Another challenge for me was that in standing, my balance was just terrible. I would have to grab on to things and Margaret would want me to stand without holding on to *anything*. I'd grab for whatever was in reach and often, the thing I grabbed was her hair as she would be next to me holding me, helping me. We would laugh about it and we figured that by the time I got through the program she would probably not have any hair left on the top of her head.

She tried to improve my balance with sturdy wooden boxes that she had. Some were 3 feet by 3 feet and they came in 3, 4 or 5 inch heights. I would have to stand in front of the boxes, facing them, and using my bad foot first, I would do step-ups and step-downs. That was probably the hardest exercise of all since my balance was so bad. I hated those boxes. I dreaded it when she pulled out those boxes. Up I would go, although grabbing on to Margaret for help, and she would say "No Betty, leave your hand down." That was the hardest thing to do because you automatically grab onto something when you feel you're about to fall. Not wanting to lose any more hair over it, Margaret finally put a box of Kleenex in my hand and strangely enough, that seemed to help my balance. So perhaps my balance was more in my

mind than anywhere else. So long as I was holding that Kleenex box, I could do the exercise well and would not grab onto her hair. Oh, but I really dreaded those "box days."

Soon we were on to walking and that took some getting used to. My balance gradually got better, although it did take time. Of course when I walked, Margaret would be with me in case I fell because my balance was still off.

Another exercise was side-stepping. I would take five steps to one side, then five steps back, grabbing at Margaret's hair the whole time. That poor lady.

I also did the stairs, which were different than the dreaded boxes. The stairs had six steps up one side and six down the other, so up and over I'd go. It was a great workout that left me sweating and puffing.

A difficult, but fun exercise, was to stand up and then sit down on a huge kind of beach ball. I would balance myself there from side-to-side and back to front and we would do that for quite a while. This was to strengthen my stomach muscles which it sure did because it required a lot of effort to pull yourself around that ball. There were many such different exercises but the one we consistently worked at was the walk. We did that every day. Learning to walk again was the single most important exercise I was to do. I always had a safety belt on but even so I was terrified of falling. Margaret always assured me she'd never let me fall and she never did.

At first, using a wooden cane, I'd go short distances, each time taking a few more steps. Soon I was walking twenty to thirty feet and was getting in the swing of it, although I had to be careful as my right leg, which was the paralyzed one, would give way if I didn't lock my knee. I found I couldn't talk when walking as I was too busy telling myself, "Step, lock and step."

Every day we practiced walking. Today, I'm still walking more with a quad-cane – still not long distances but I'm working on it each day. In the hospital I couldn't use the treadmill or the bars as I only had one hand to hold on with.

My weekdays were busy, but weekends could get quite boring as there was no therapy; however, my family were wonderful and they would come in often and Bill, of course, would come in whenever he could. I was very lucky to have my daughter Pat, who was teaching in Red Deer, come in every day during the week, and on weekends she would return to Carbon. For months, she would come in to see me daily. That was wonderful. Kelly, Judy and Beth would come to see me whenever they could, even coloring my hair for me.

Coloring my hair was a real riot! Since I couldn't stand at the sink, I had to sit in my wheelchair and bend my head back. Some of the girls held a basin of water under my head with the other pouring water over it. I said, "Gosh, I should just go grey out." But I was told, "It wouldn't be you, Mom." Several nurses came in and we were all laughing so hard – there was enough water on the floor to flow into the Nile and I was soaking wet. But the end result was perfect. In fact, some nurses asked for the brand and number!

During the week, therapy kept me so busy that I didn't have time for some of the other programs at the hospital. Church was every Wednesday and sing-songs were held at various times during the week. But as I have said, most of these I could not participate in since I was in therapy, which is what I was there for! Whenever I did have a rare opportunity to do other activities, I would take part in whatever was available.

There were many wonderful volunteers in the activities programs. One, I think his name was Hugh, kept us occupied with all sorts of creative events. He would arrange special meals, to which he would invite various patients. These were exclusive, invitation-only events and while you may not get to attend every one, he made sure everybody had a chance to take part. It was a wonderful feeling when he would come around and invite you to the next event and you never knew what it was going to be. These meals included hotcake breakfasts, fish and chip lunches and supper pizza parties. It was always something different. He would come into your room and invite you to one of these special occasion meals, then he would check your calendar and make your reservation.

He also had a news discussion time once a week when we would sit at a huge, round table and hash over the headlines for that week. We were all stroke victims. Some of the answers were amazing and everyone took it very seriously. It was a real "Knights of the Round Table" meeting. The knights were in all types of regalia of hospital gown – some gowns left wide open, some people with ball caps on. The people were as varied as the topics we discussed. Some got very angry if their viewpoints were not accepted: "I said it was Ottawa!" slamming a hand down. I think King Arthur would have been proud!

There were also a few Church Ministers I got to know well. One especially had a marvelous singing voice and would have sing-songs including many Irish and Scottish folk songs. He had a small group who would sing with him. One time, as I was being wheeled back after therapy, we passed by the room where the Minister and his friends were having a program and all were in full song. The room was full and everyone was singing with great gusto – not always the same song. I was wheeled to the back of the room and the funniest thing happened although it was almost sad. As I was wheeled in, he noticed me and announced that a very famous singer, "Betty Kilgour," and her friend were prepared to sing a song. Suddenly I was wheeled to the front of the room. Well, I had never sang in my life! Fortunately, he sang with us and the other lady could carry a tune. The stroke had taken my voice, so all I could contribute was a croak. The song was "My Ain Folk" and as the Scottish folk know, this is a very sad song as they are crying for their Ain Folk back home. So we sang this sad song, me doing my best. I knew some of the words, but it was pathetic, believe me! I looked into the crowd, noticed some people crying and thought, *Oh this is really bad.* But when we finished, we received many compliments, with some people saying that it made them homesick. I thought they must have been having trouble with their hearing, but I had got through my first public performance! There were many things like this that kept me occupied and happy.

We also had other church ministers who would volunteer at the hospital and I got to know them well. They would stop into our rooms, for a chat, to cheer us up and say a little prayer before they left. Talking about prayers, it was prayers that kept me going the whole time I was there. In fact I prayed so much I imagined God was up there saying, "Oh no, not that woman again." That was what kept me going when I was down though, because I knew that prayer would comfort and cheer me up. So to anyone in a similar position of ill-health, for goodness sake grab onto God's hand and hold on!

I should tell you a bit about the meals. The regular meals were really very good. Some people complained of course, but I could see no reason at all. I always felt hungry especially in the evenings, so I had my girls bring me cookies. I would ask for a cup of tea before I went to sleep and would have some of those cookies. Of course, for me, cookies are like salted peanuts and once I started eating them I couldn't stop. I used to eat so many, that it became a joke among the nurses and they would tease me when they would see three packets of Dads cookies on my shelf every night and another half empty one on my table.

The nursing staff were wonderful. There were many changes, of course, and while there were a great variety of nurses, I got to know them so well. They would tell me stories of their families, boyfriends and various other relationships. I loved it when they popped in to see me. A lot of the nurses were from the Philippines. One of them was there after my hair had been colored by my daughters and she was quite taken by it, so she went home and dyed her hair the same color. Now of course, her hair was jet black and mine is reddish-brown, so it didn't have quite the same result but it did still look very pretty on her. Some of the girls wanted their hair like mine. At this stage my hair was really curly, which it had turned after my stroke. I told them all they needed to do was to have a stroke to achieve the same look! They figured it wasn't worth it.

The nurses would also come to test my perfume and would remark on me applying makeup every day asking if I was vain. I said, "No not vain, it just makes me feel better". I would do everything I could to make myself feel better each day.

There was one lady named Jackie whose title was Recreational Therapist for Acute Care. She did many things there making sure everyone was kept busy and happy. She did her job very well. Jackie would drop by my room just out of the blue and was a very cheerful, upbeat person with an effervescent personality. If I was ever feeling a little down, I would call her and she would pop in and help me get over it. Depression is part and parcel of having a stroke and it is up to you how you deal with it. Really you have to deal with it strongly or you go under. Anyway, Jackie was very good at cheering people up and she thought I should have some sort of handiwork to do. Well having only one hand that worked was going to make this difficult, but in the shops where the therapies were going on, they would make different little things for patient needs. I needed something to hold a ball of wool, so she had them make me a "thing" – like for the old-fashioned spool, where you slip the thread over 5 or so nails. This was made for me on a much larger scale, about the size of a dinner plate. There were little pegs all around it and she would cast the stitches on to it and then I would do it with my good hand using a knitting needle to slip the thread over. I actually got some knitting done on it! Jackie was a wonderful person.

Once, when busy with my spool-knitting contraption, the pastor from our church in Three Hills, Minister Ryan, came in to see me. I told him I was going to make something out of it and he said that if I did, he would wear it. Well then I just had to take up the dare. So I got the most vivid pink and green I could find, with Jackie's help of course, and made up a kind of toque. I gave it to him and he even wore it to church which was quite amazing. I wish I had been there to see it but they did take pictures.

Another time, a wonderful surprise was when Pastor Ryan and his wife Juanita, came to see me on St. Patrick's Day. They brought me green cake, green jelly and croissants, all sorts of other goodies, a "Top of the Morning" hat and shamrocks – the whole bit. These are the kinds of things which cheered me up as we went along.

Most of the patients would go home on home leave for overnights on the weekends. I was not able to at this stage for neither I, nor my house, were ready for it. So that was to come and that is what I worked toward.

One day Jackie came down to see me and she said, "Betty, we would be really honored if you could speak to the nursing students at the Red Deer College on our behalf this year." It seems that each year, one of the stroke patients would be taken to the college to answer questions and if you could speak, then you would be invited to speak to the class. I thought, *My goodness, I have just had a stroke, so how could I possibly do that?* My voice was croaking and everything, but I thought about it, as I had always loved public speaking. I did some deep thinking and finally I thought, *Why not try?* So, I contacted Jackie again and told her that I would give it a whirl.

But the day before the event, I was talking to someone when I gave an immense sneeze and my upper denture flew out, over and sailed onto the bed. It just flew out so unexpectedly. I got to thinking, *I can't go and speak in case my teeth fall out!* So I had another friend who came in to visit me, get me some Polygrip and I had to use that to make my teeth more firm. I was then willing to give it a try, but I imagined my teeth suddenly flying across the platform. Being as how my voice gets croaky fairly quickly, I asked a friend to buy me a bottle of Buckleys which I took along in a brown bag. I would take a slug of it every once in a while and I managed to speak to them without too much difficulty, but there I was, hoping my teeth wouldn't fly out, and drinking from a paper bag!

The students seemed interested in my stories of Africa, a topic I had often spoken on during my public speaking engagements before my stroke. I told them that when they are nursing stroke patients, remember to be gracious with them and to try to cheer them up since we are often feeling down enough. This seemed to go over well.

To be able to speak to a group of people just months after having had a stroke, gave me a huge sense of accomplishment. I felt good and it gave me hope for the future that I would be able to continue with public speaking engagements. I don't know if I will, but it is an encouraging thought.

Although I was kept ver, busy with therapy, I was always looking out for ways to fill what little spare time I had. With the therapy, I felt I was slowly getting stronger and I rather looked forward to it. My occupational therap, continued with the concentration on my arm and involving many different exercises. It was a great source of joy – for me, the nurses and my girls – whenever I managed to get even a very small amount of movement back into my fingers. These little movements kept me going and gave me much encouragement. Speech therapy followed for another hour, back to "Me, me, me" and all sorts of other cadences, then back to my room for dinner. And then, around 2:00 or 3:00 p.m., I would go down to physiotherapy with Margaret. I was getting stronger as a result and was walking further. I was now using a cane. This was good although sometimes very tiring. Sometimes I would say that I could not do it but Margaret would say "Yes, you can." Off we would go, and I'd do it. We would walk various distances first around the room, then around the whole hall way. The therapy always involved a big "distance" walk and many other smaller exercises in between which Margaret felt were equally important. They were very important because they strengthened me. Every time I went a little further, or did something well, I went back to my room feeling elated and Margaret would be happy for me. My one goal still was to get back home to Bill. While Bill was busy fixing the house, I was busy trying to do my part, fixing me!

Four

Making Adjustments

One day, near the end of my time in the program, I had a terrible pain in my rib cage. It was a weekend and there were no doctors around. The pain was truly dreadful. It felt as though the rib I had broken previously had broken again. Margaret and I had really been working hard on the mat the day before. She had been teaching me how to get off the floor in case of a fall. It had been a tough workout and I wondered if I had cracked my rib again. All the nurses could do was to give me Tylenol. By the Monday morning, the pain had become unbearable. It was then I noticed a strange line of blisters under my bust line. I realized what my problem was – shingles. At least, that's what I thought it was. When my doctor came in, he confirmed my suspicions and put me immediately onto some antiviral drugs and cream. It even hurt to lie on my side as I also had some rashes on my back, but it was deep in my rib cage that it really hurt. I know shingles are caused by some virus and stress but I did not really feel stressed out. And so here I was, at the end of my therapy, with shingles and no home care worker in sight. *What more?* I thought. I soon found out.

The doctor came in a few days later and formally announced that I was through the therapy, but also stated he could not send me home without a home care worker. So he was going to be sending me to the Three Hills Hospital, where they had room for me. I was to leave the very next day. Well by now my hope was up, but it came down with this surprise. I think my shingles hurried things on a bit.

The next day, my girls came and packed me up, which was quite a job as I had collected quite a bit of stuff during my seven month hospital stay. One thing that had given me the greatest joy while in hospital was my collection of music cassettes. I had quite a good collection of tapes, mainly Irish folk songs and some hymns. These I played every day and only once was I asked to turn them down. Sometimes Margaret would come and borrow a couple and we would work out to them. Music heals the heart and soul and I can't live without it. So the hospital rang with rollicking tunes during my stay.

My goodbyes were very sad, particularly leaving all of my therapists with whom I spent so much time and had come to love. But I was happy to be going to my hometown of Three Hills, and back to my own wonderful doctor, family and friends. It was a lovely spring day to be driving out in the countryside and to be outside again after all those months in the hospital. I had spent the whole winter in the hospital and now I was out.

Soon I was settled in the Three Hills Hospital, waiting for Bill to find a home-care worker who could live in. Every day I would go to therapy, so I would still remain as mobile as possible. The therapy was a little different, my new therapist, Berend, was a dear and a tall handsome Dutch man! He had immigrated to Canada a number of years before. He had such a great sense of humor, which immediately endeared him to me. Berend was wonderful to work with, pushing me to the limit and often leaving me puffing like a steam engine.

I kept giving it my all, wanting to stay as strong as possible for when I did go home. The days went by slowly. Bill put an advertisement in the *Calgary Herald* for home care, as I had been told that I would soon be placed in some long term care unit, because there was no room for me at the hospital. I did not want that. All this time, my shingles were still troubling me as they were very painful.

Then one wonderful day, Bill came bustling into my room, a grin on his handsome face.

"Betty, I think we have a helper. You don't mind if it's a man do you?"

I replied, "Honey, I have had many male nurses during my seven months in hospital and they were all wonderful. Of course I don't mind!"

Bill told me that he had a letter from a young man from the Philippines who was a home care specialist. He wanted work and Bill planned to meet him the next day! I thought straight away that I could now go home. The day I had worked so hard for was at hand.

All of a sudden I was scared. My home in Three Hills was comparatively new to me, as I had only lived in it for five months prior to my stroke. Bill and I had lived on the land that Bill's father had homesteaded in 1905. In fact, we had all lived in the house that Bill was born in. There we raised our five children and had lived very happily for all those years. We had years filled with hilarity, happiness, crops, hired men, droughts, calving, haying, lots of love and laughter, and our share of sorrow and sunshine. After fifty-four years, we decided it was time to leave the farm and let our son take over. It was certainly a huge change, moving from the farm into town, even though the farm was only two miles away.

It was the move from farm life to town life that was really the big change. A lot of our friends did, of course, live in town and we could still go to our own church, Bethel Fellowship, which was near our farm. So really it was not that big of a change. Bill had said to the girls and me, "Go to town and find a house." We went through the local paper, made a few phone calls, found a wonderful real estate agent who knew what we wanted and who really helped us. He arranged some viewings for us. I do have a habit, which annoys my family, of wanting everything done yesterday or at least today! We spent days going through homes. I wanted a home that would accommodate our ever increasing family – particularly the front room – and enough guest rooms for our friends and in-laws who would stay over night. Those were my two stipulations. We viewed all available, turning down one after another. We finally found one and it was lovely, with a great front room, kitchen and all the guest rooms I would need. It was wonderful. We hurried home to tell Bill. He agreed that it would be a fine home in a great location – not far from downtown and not too many stairs.

And so it was time for the big move. Fifty-four years of "stuff." Not that I collected everything, because I can dump stuff with the greatest of ease, but still there was a lot we had accumulated over the years.

Being such a short move, just the two miles, we didn't have to pack too carefully. Every time someone went into town, they would take a box or two. Then the day of the big move came. I told the girls to unpack in the new home, putting everything wherever they thought it should go, so I was really unpacked even before I moved into town! When I arrived, the beds were made and everything was ready. Then the settling in began.

I had a neat little area in the back garden which had some perennials in it. So I transplanted some plants from the farm to the new residence. I was thrilled to find a huge pink rose bush and even a raspberry patch. But my best find was an old fashioned lilac bush, the ones that smell so heavenly. I visited all the local greenhouses and filled all my flower boxes, and so we settled into our new lives. I liked my house and all our friends around us. Sure, I missed the farm, particularly cutting the grass, which may sound strange, but I loved that job. It was a joy for me to sit upon my big old lawn mower and cut the large area of grass that we had. It could take three or four hours to do, but I loved it. My lawn in town would not be able to handle such a mower, so I had to look for other sources of amusement.

We were very fortunate to have wonderful neighbors. A Dutch couple, Harry and Ally, were so kind to us. They were always dropping in with some home-made goodies and home-grown delicacies. Another neighbor was Brian. He was a dear old friend from bygone years. The rest of the neighbors, we are still hoping to get to know.

Summer ran into fall, visitors came from overseas and a grandson's wedding took place. Then in November, all was well, when the unthinkable happened and I had this massive stroke. I thought strokes were for old people and I don't think of myself as being all that ancient, but I had a *dandy*.

The stroke took me away from Bill, my new home, every one I held dear, and pushed me into a strange, new life. Now I was about to return home, therapy completed, and I was scared. Could I really do it? Bill was on his way to Calgary to pick up my live-in caregiver. Little did I know that such a wonderful person was going to be playing such a big role in my life.

Five

A Whole New Life

The girls came in and packed me up again. The good-byes to the nurses and everyone were not so sad this time. I knew I would be seeing the staff often, as I would continue to go into the hospital for therapy and blood tests, so I sat in the hospital room, waiting nervously for Bill's return. Finally he showed up with this small, young man with a dazzling smile, who came straight up to my wheelchair, gently took my hand and said "Hello Miss Betty, I am Paulo." From that moment on, I was Miss Betty. He immediately, picked up my bags and boxes and took them to the car. I was soon being wheeled out and I wondered if I was going to be able to transfer to the car since I had not practiced this for a while. But Paulo wheeled me right up to the car door, led me though the motions and we did wonderfully well. Soon we were in the back yard and I was helped out of the car (Paulo and I have perfected the motions and now are a matched pair), then onto the lift that Bill had installed and up onto the deck. My flower boxes, which Ian had planted while I was away, were in full bloom. Tears streamed down my face. I could not hold them back. I was home. I had hoped and prayed for this moment during my seven months and now, here I was.

Paulo proved to be totally amazing. Part of his story is told in Appendix B. He seems to know my every need and to be able to do everything so efficiently and kindly. One big chore is to look after my daily pill consumption and keeping them all straight is quite a job since I take an amazing amount – I think about twenty-five every day. One pill I take, which is an ongoing one is Prednisone. It causes a great deal of weight gain and ballooning in the face and shoulders. In fact, the ballooning in my face is so great, I haven't seen my cheekbones in months. It also causes great bruising on my arms for little or no reason. Most times I look like I have gone ten rounds with Mike Tyson. It is one I would dearly love to get rid of. Anyway, if they are helping me stay healthy, I don't mind.

I just can't say enough about Paulo. He not only looks after me totally, he also does all the cooking and cleaning in his wonderful way and looks after Bill, who is continuously on oxygen. He does all this with great efficiency and kindness. Paulo's a great cook. At first I felt as though I had to sit in the kitchen to pass him tips on how to cook, but he has got so good, he now just wheels me into the front room while he does it on his own.

With Paulo living with us, our new lives took form. We formed new routines slowly and easily and best of all I was home again. We had lots of company which was great as I love to have visitors. When I felt as though I needed more company, I would phone a friend to come around for a cup of tea.

With Paulo's help, I was getting more settled in my new life. I started off using a borrowed wheelchair from the Red Deer hospital, but when I finally got my own it was so much better. I could spin on a dime and back up and maneuver. I had not been getting out much, so one day Paulo decided we should go on an outing to the downtown. He pushed me the whole seven blocks which was a bit much, but oh, it was so good to be out in the sunshine and it was neat to look into all the stores. We did this a couple of times, but it was not fair on Paulo. It was just too far and the were too many curbs to climb, so we quit that.

At this time, I wanted very much to get back to my church. The elders had one time brought me communion, but I still wanted to get back. I must tell you, I would never have got through my stroke without my faith in God. *No* way. It carried me through and still does. On Sunday, Bill thought that we could try to make a trip to our church. The weather was fine and everything was reasonable. I wondered where I would sit in the church in my wheelchair and thought I could sit behind the pulpit if necessary! So off we all went and arrived in good time. By this time, Paulo and I had a made a science out of maneuvering in and out of the car. So up the church ramp I went, and was greeted by the church family. I sat in the aisle comfortably and we have been going almost every Sunday since. Now when I want or need to go downtown, Paulo or Bill gets me to the lift in the back garden, out into the car, and Bill drives us all downtown. When we're ready to go back home, we reverse the whole process. It has been working very well.

One strange affliction due to my stroke is quite amusing and even happens in church. This yawning. Yes, I said yawning! Not little ladylike yawns but great gaping ones. They are not caused by tiredness and they hit me any time, day or night and any place, no matter where I am. In church, which is utterly embarrassing, I'll be hit by a bout of yawns. I don't just have one or two either, but can have up to ten or more in a row. I could be visiting with Queen Elizabeth or the Pope and I'd still have yawning bouts. When we have friends in, no matter how interesting they are, off I'll go and they get worried they've played me out which I have to try to explain. It's just a reflex action. So if you see me in a stroke of yawning as big as the Boulder Dam, don't worry. I'm not tired out or bored. It's just another interesting part of my stroke.

Since I had not shopped for seven months, I really enjoyed being able to visit the shops again. My three regular stops were SAAN, Fields and IDA Drugs. One day I noted some nice blue sneakers, which I thought would be ideal for me at home. So I went to the store and bought three pairs, even though my walking was limited to just one room at home. They did look a little bit different but they were on sale. One day, one of my daughters dropped in and saw my new shoes. She didn't say anything to me, but later she saw one of the health nurses downtown and told her "We don't need to worry about Mum slipping in the shower, she has just bought three pairs of sand shoes!"

"How often does she plan to shower?" the nurse asked.

I had not realized that these shoes were to be used at the beach. I must admit they do work wonderfully well in the shower. The first pair is not showing any wear yet.

One beautiful gift I had received on my return home was a male canary from Bill. It was not singing too much at first, but he did try so hard. He would puff up his chest and cheep away. His chest would almost burst with the effort. He has since learned to sing so well, that sometimes people will ask if I can turn him off. I even heard someone suggest that we could roast him. Imagine that! Now Bill is getting used to hearing aids and the singing is driving him crazy as it is so loud. But I love the bird's singing. It brings so much joy to the home.

Every day, Paulo exercises my useless arm. The odd time, my fingers will move a tiny bit but nothing substantial, but I am not giving up. Also every morning, I walk with my cane as far as I can and once a week, I go to the hospital to a therapist there, where he makes me walk with the cane or a walker. The walker was new to me. I have to stand straight, put both arms in slots and hang onto the brake handle for dear life. It is quite a workout, but one which I enjoy. He also has me going up and down a couple of stairs but it is still a challenge and one that I am slowly getting used to doing. I really do enjoy my therapy as he challenges me. When I balk or say that I can't do something, he will say, "Yes you can, Betty," and I usually can!

When I first got home, I had not felt ready to step out socially. I was not sure how I was going to be accepted as an invalid. I actually did not feel like an invalid, but I was still a little bit scared inside, as I wondered how people would react to me now, but going out socially was another step I would have to take. One of my grandsons was going to be married and there was a shower for his fiancée in a small town just outside of Three Hills. I really wanted to go so I got dressed up, my girls got me into the car and off we went. All was wheelchair accessible, so I got in fine. All my daughters were there and so were many of my granddaughters – and lots of friends. In that atmosphere, I felt just like everyone else. It was a great evening and I got over the feeling of being different. I now felt comfortable going to any occasion. I was accepted everywhere I went.

Paulo, being on duty day and night, has some time off each month. His favorite place to visit is Calgary, where his fiancée, Sally lives. She is the cutest little girl and we just love her as we do Paulo. She is a pretty little thing and is Nanny for children in that city. I go into the respite room in our hospital on Paulo's days off. It is just a little room, kept for people like me, who need help all the time. It is part of the Extended Care program offered at our hospital.

I was not sure if I wanted to be there with so many old people who are so ill or mentally troubled but I had no alternative. To my delight, when I got there, I quite enjoyed it. I knew most of the nurses and staff and they are a wonderful group of people. The nurses work so hard joshing the patients that it is lively and fun. Some patients are in wheelchairs and some are quite with it, while others are off somewhere else – but even they can be entertaining. One fellow, a former farmer, will say to me "We have got half the combining done and will do the rest tomorrow. How is Bill doing?" It is lots of fun. I always tell people when I am going there, that in fact I am going to my spa. They also have lots of entertainment. Bingo, wheelchair volleyball, sing-songs and church. I do try to attend as many things as possible even though the sing-songs are quite bad. When I had my stroke, it affected my vocal chords. Even though I had never been able to sing well, I had enjoyed singing a lot. But now all I could offer up was a croak. It is terrible. I sing anyway.

I love the staff. They take much abuse from the patients: grouching about the food, or complaining that they are not being fed quickly enough, but the staff take it all in their stride. One neat thing in there are the birds. They have three cockatoos. One old friend who stays at the centre has tamed them. They now ride about with him on his walker handles, or on his shoulders or even on his walking stick. He can set them onto anyone's shoulder as well.

A big incentive to stay optimistic is that the food is good. Hot and tasty! I heard that the cook used to work at the Banff Springs Hotel. His presentation of the food adds to the great taste.

Another neat outing for me, is the Three Hills annual parade, which passes just a few blocks from our home. So Bill, Paulo and I, went to see it. Some friends also came over – some I had not seen since I went into the hospital. The parade was much the same as always: horses, kids, bands and floats. Paulo who had seen many parades back in the Philippines, enjoyed seeing the Western version. He even ran out to pick up the candy that was thrown from the passing floats, encouraged by me of course! This was a way to get a supply for all the little children who come to visit me.

Another event I wanted to attend was a book launching. Another dear friend had recently finished his book on his African adventures. He had been born there and had become a well known guide and outfitter, having even taken out Prince Bernhardt of the Netherlands on safaris many times and with who he was good friends. This world is a small place and one illustration of this is that Bill, Beth and I had spent two years in Tanzania. Our headquarters were at Sumbawanga, located in the deep south-west part of the country. It is so remote, most people have never heard of it, let alone ever visited there. When we returned to Three Hills, I started writing books. I returned to Sumbawanga a number of times and wrote a book on one of my trips, called *Sumbawanga Safari*. The books were sold at a local Three Hills store.

One day a little lady came into the store and loudly expressed her delight at seeing them. She enquired from the store person who had written them. Well the store person was a friend of mine, so she could share my details with the customer. Not long after, I got a phone call from a man speaking Swahili of all things. This man was Eric Balston, the author of the book I wanted to attend the launching for. It turned out that this little woman who just happened upon my book, out of the blue, was Mrs. Balston, wife of the author whose book launching I so wanted to attend! For such a strange thing to happen is rare when you consider that Sumbawanga is to Africa what a tiny rural town is to Canada: a warm and wonderful place to call home, but just a dot on the map in the bigger picture! The amazing thing out of all this was that Eric had been the head gamekeeper at Sumbawanga for some eight years, about six years before we had lived there! Now he was living in Linden, about twenty miles from us and had written a book about his own adventures.

I really wanted to be at the launch. I didn't know if I could be, as I did not know if the place would have wheelchair access. I did get a call from him one day, since he knew how much I wanted to attend. "Betty, there is a lift there. It is broken, but I will fix it." I had another call from him saying that it was working, all it had needed was a bolt and now it worked fine. "Wonderful," I exclaimed. So off we went on launch day and Eric was waiting there to greet us. I got onto the lift, which creaked a bit, but it worked fine. I managed to sit for four hours in my wheelchair watching some wonderful wildlife movies that he had taken. Some were so close that it made you gasp. I could even see the flies on the Wildebeest heads. What a wonderful afternoon it was.

The first year rolled on. I got stronger and would sometimes test my strength out. This sometimes got me into trouble. Just this week, Bill and Paulo had gone downtown for groceries while I was at home in my wheelchair. Now we do this all the time and I am fine, but this time, I needed to go the bathroom. I mean, I *really* had to go. So I thought to myself, *I can do it*. I wheeled myself into the bathroom, right up to the pole. I lifted up my foot pedal and stood up and just hung on. I got my jeans down and sat down feeling quite smug. I thought maybe I should just sit there when I was finished instead of getting back into my wheelchair and just wait for Paulo to return, but the wheelchair was right there and I was sure I could do it. So I got up, stepped over to my wheelchair and reached down but felt I could not properly sit down as the angle was bad. So I took a couple of steps over and attempted to sit down on the chair. The wheelchair shot out from under me and I was left sitting on a couple of inches of the seat! I had forgotten to set the brakes and there I was hanging on for dear life. I thought I had better slide onto the floor and so I ended up on the floor, spread out like a beached whale. I tried to adjust my body to an element of comfort and wondered how long I was going to have to lie there. I tried to get my good leg under me, but to no avail. I lay there for about thirty minutes that felt much longer but I was not hurt and felt that I would be fine if I could try it again. Next time I'll remember the brake!

When the men arrived, I was helped up and although I was fine, I was a little bit shaken. The next day, though I was stiff and had quite a collection of bruises, I was pleased that I had been able to get to the bathroom. I would just have to be more careful next time and remember the brakes. Funny to be proud of something that had ended with me sitting on the floor, but I was.

Another social event I managed to attend was a Robbie Burns night at the United Church in town. Some friends invited us, but it was to be held in the church basement and I knew I was not going to be able to walk down the steps. But they told me there was a lift and that it would be able to carry me down the steps. I thought that was wonderful. When we arrived, Bill, Paulo and I went up the ramp and into the church vestibule to get onto the lift. My wheelchair was bolted down and I was told to lie back until I was almost horizontal. Soon I was chugging down the stairs, sounding like a tractor bulldozer. I reached the basement safely which had been all decorated in true Scottish tradition. It was a wonderful evening. The Haggis, the main delicacy of every Robbie Burns banquet, was duly 'piped in' with a bagpiper in full Scottish dress leading the way with the steaming Haggis carried in behind him. The address to the Haggis was even performed by a real Scotchman, who then cut it with a huge sword about the size of a good hoe. The dish, with steam rolling out of its innards was then taken to the kitchen, prepared for serving and soon afterward we were digging into it. There were good Scottish songs and much dancing. I absorbed it all like a sponge. I never worried for a minute about being in a wheelchair.

One thing that did happen there, which was alarming at the time, but which I have laughed a lot about since, was related to the trouble I have getting to the bathroom on time, especially for a bowel movement. Now I always try to time it but on that night, even though I had gone earlier during the day, I was caught with an urgent need. The toilet was up two stairs and I panicked. Paulo of course was with me but those two steps looked like Mount Kilimanjaro. Two men lifted up my wheelchair onto the top of the stairs. Now I was in my panic stage. I grabbed two nurses who were there and who I knew from the hospital. So with their help and Paulo's, I was hustled into the bathroom. I laugh about it a lot now, because I seemed to have every one in there with me, except for the bagpipers and Scottish dancers! When we got home, Paulo quite sensibly said "We could have done it ourselves, Miss Betty and you could easily have walked up the two steps. Everybody in that room knew you had to go the bathroom by the time you were through."

"But Paulo, I panicked," I replied, "and you know what I'm like in panic mode." It is not a pretty sight.

When faced with new situations and things, I do tend to panic instead of thinking it through. I tend to go ballistic. I do try now to contain my panics and try to control my visits with Mother nature, but I know that this is not always possible.

I love going out for a meal at a restaurant but I knew some in town were not wheelchair accessible but ever since I came home I'd heard about a new place in town. My friends would ask, "Betty, have you been to the Tea House? It's really neat." "Mom, they serve lovely food, even Chappatis, Samosis and Chi." Ah, shades of my old African days.

"Oh, I probably can't get in," I said.

By this time, I was feeling sorry for myself – some of my kids had already been there, so I had Bill check if there was a wheelchair ramp. Sure enough, he told me they had a good one. So one day, Bill, Paulo and I decided to go to the Nilgris Tea House for lunch. It was only about three blocks from our house, but I was in great expectation as I had heard so much about it.

As I was wheeled in the door, my eyes were drawn to a huge colored map of India on the wall and a lovely collection of China cups and saucers on display. The restaurant proved to be small but cozy. The patrons and staff were so warm and friendly that I need not have worried about the wheelchair. There was lots of room for it. I can't remember what I ate, but I do remember how much at home I felt and now it's one of our favorite eating spots.

I'm learning not to be afraid to try any venture, wheelchair or not. Of course, none of my ventures would be possible without Paulo. In fact, it was at the Tea House I had another adventure.

I'm absolutely paranoid about having to go to public washrooms, especially if they don't have a handrail in them. So one time, I was caught needing to go when at the Tea House but Paulo who saves me so many times, took over. He knows I get myself in a state, so this time he just said, "You can do it, Miss Betty," wheeling me to the door, giving me orders like an army sergeant.

"Stand up!

"Take four steps now!

"Two backward!

"Sit down!"

It went so smoothly, I couldn't believe it. It's really silly but I'm so pleased with every small achievement. *Now*, I thought, *I can go to a public bathroom!*

Talking about going out, one of my greatest joys is to go shopping. I like shopping for anything – even parts for Bill's machinery when we lived on the farm, but now the habit has been strictly curtailed, my stroke has seen to that. I do get downtown now and again but not all stores are wheelchair accessible. It is hard shopping from a wheelchair but I still have fun and the store staff are so helpful. I even enjoy going to my bank to withdraw money. Am I a lunatic or what?

I have found a wonderful new shopping venue which I have used for years but never to the extent I do now and that is the Sears catalogue. It is so much fun. Almost every page has something which I desperately want. It is so easy, I can phone in myself to place the order if Paulo is busy. Bill is beginning to wonder, as just about every week we get a call from Sears saying that there is a parcel there for me. It is almost as good as shopping at the store. You can return things for a full refund immediately and in that way I get to try clothes and take it back right away. Bill thinks there is a special path worn out from our house to Sears. It is great fun and I thoroughly enjoy it. Last Christmas I did all my shopping through the Sears Wish List and I do a *lot* of shopping at Christmas. I had a real ball. Some families did get some odd gifts due to my strange sense of humor.

I just love to shop. Now that the Spring and Summer catalogues are out again, I have a lot more shopping ahead of me.

Not so long ago, I needed some new brassieres. I had not been able to wear any since my shingles and with the weight gain from the Prednisone, I now needed a larger size. So Kelly, Paulo and I decided to go shopping in another town. Kelly had given me a gift certificate and I wanted a new dress for a granddaughter's upcoming wedding. It was a big adventure for me, so off we all went.

When we came to get the brassieres, it was a riot. I kept telling the salesperson, that I took a 36C. She said that I did not, because she took that size and she was much smaller. "I *know*," she said. "I have been selling these for years and you are no 36C!" She measured me and a knowing look was on her face. She did not say anything and I kept on with my insistence that I was that size. "There are none here that are your size," she sniffed, "but I will look upstairs for you."

She returned with a box that was big enough to hold a baler canvass. She pulled out the contents for me to try it on. The wheelchair would not fit into the dressing room, but I had to try the brassiere to make sure it fit. I stripped off in the corner, with Paulo holding up my jacket. The lady came at with me with a white thing that looked like a tent with enough number-9 wire to have fenced the south forty. It was ridiculous but I got the sales woman to try it on me. It was terrible but I bought one anyway. I paid for it, but as the saleswoman gave me the change, she gave it to me with a smirk on her face. On the way home, I was still curious about the odd exchange.

"Kelly, what size did I ask for?

"36C," she replied.

"Oh my goodness!" I exclaimed. "I take a 46 C. Why did I tell her a 36C?"

That poor lady, she had really earned her pay that day and I had been so adamant. *Oh well*, I thought, *blame it on the stroke!*

In my new life, when I need a hair cut, I call a hairdresser who makes house calls. "Have blower, will travel" kind of thing. When I need color, Paulo's wife Sally or one of my girls will do it, and my nails, the same thing. I feel so pampered. I just sit back in my levered armchair, which Bill and the kids bought for me, and wallow in my pampering. One thing I have trouble with is my tailbone getting sore. So Paulo found some egg carton foam and now I perch on it like a sitting hen and it has really helped.

One wonderful thing that the stroke brought about, if there is such a thing, is that a lot of our kin come to visit now. Maybe now that we have to stay put, it's easier for them to find us at home! Bill's two sisters, as well as his brother and his brother's wife, will come for several days at a time which I really love. I am someone who loves her in-laws. I see much more of my own sister and brother now too, which is wonderful. I love company and we get a lot of it. When I get bored I just phone friends to come by. One day I had a phone call from a couple in the nearby town of Acme: they wanted to ask some questions about Africa. I said that would be wonderful and invited them for supper. There is a story behind this as you may have guessed.

Many years ago when Bill, Beth and I spent two years in Tanzania as volunteers, I had got to know the mainly Tanzanian staff and also the founder of our mission, orphanage and hospital. Even after we had returned to Canada, I would go back there as often as possible for a change. This story is covered in my book, *So This is Africa*. While there, I had seen the great need of the people and children and so I had been sending little parcels of baby clothes back there, maybe some booties or baby jackets. I had spent a lot of my time doing this.

This began twenty-six years ago and my work continued to grow every year. Sometimes my upstairs looked like a Salvation Army used clothing store. Friends and the Church would donate clothing and money to send the parcels off. I just loved doing it, and it was so much fun, packing all the items into little cotton bags. It was not long until we were sending 180 packages a year and growing. The story of this is in my book, *Sumbawanga Safari.* I loved this work, but after twenty-six years I was feeling the pressure, but just did not want to stop.

Then one evening, I had a niggling little feelings. I felt I should bring Moses, one of the main people from the Mission, back to Canada, to visit the churches that were helping him. It was a good idea, I thought, but did not think too seriously about it. The feeling never left me, so I later brought it up with my church group and they thought it was a good idea as well. We sent an invitation off to him and he accepted. I had his itinerary and soon he was with us. I could not believe the speed with which it all happened. We met him in Calgary and I drove him across the countryside to visit all the churches. It was fun. He was so well received and they all loved him. He proved to us, by being here and telling us in his own words instead of through the long-distance correspondence we were both used to, just how much our help was needed.

After he left, I again felt the whole Kilangala project was getting too big, but I could not let it go now. Moses had suggested that we form a board and I mulled the idea around in my mind for several days. Finally, I phoned a few friends I thought were very capable and more importantly, had a deep love for Kilangala in their hearts. We gathered in my living room and the *Friends Of Kilangala Board* was formed. I told them I did not want to sit on the board as I felt they would do better without me. I felt wonderful about it, sure that this board with its new innovations and ideas would sail better without me. Although I did feel a bit melancholy at the time, a load was lifted from my shoulders. Then just a matter of weeks after the board formed, I had my stroke. I am sure

God had it all planned. I was awestruck with the timing as I lay there in my hospital bed.

The board really worked well. It flew with them. They did everything, even collecting enough funds for a container which they also packed with some farm equipment. There were all sorts of school supplies sent for the village schools which are always short of material and they are always thrilled when a bunch of pencils and scribblers come. There were a lot of supplies for the orphanage as well.

The orphanage is there because in that remote part of Tanzania where the Kilangala mission is, there are *many* orphans. There is malaria in that area.When pregnant mothers catch it, the result is a death sentence 80% of the time. The mothers will deliver their babies and then pass away from the malaria. If there is no mother in the village to take care of the baby, they have to get the baby to the mission where the orphanage is. If they can't get there, the babies die. So Kilangala always has a collection of orphans and as I have said, a lot of the material sent was for the orphanage.

Kilangala is the name of the mission which is about twelve miles from the town of Sumbawanga. After sending the container, a Board member and his wife were sent over to see if there were any improvements in how we could send the material. Paul and Rita went over and they were great Ambassadors to send. They returned with great news that all was going well and how much our contributions were appreciated. And now at this time, the amazing thing is that a whole group of people from the town of Acme who had been helping with the project, are planning to go over at Christmas for a working holiday. They hope to lay some piping to get water to the orphanage and to work on some buildings.

The group is made up of men, women and young nursing students who are interested in the hospital there. Some are hoping they'll be able to stay on after the group leaves.

I am so thrilled that the whole project has grown to this stage. Some of the couples who are going to be making the trip in December wanted now to come see Bill and me to ask some questions about what to expect, what to take with them and what to wear. It was a wonderful evening and we talked so much that I was hoarse. A few weeks later a group of the young nursing students came around and we had a wonderful time with them – they were delightful. I just can't believe it has grown so large, just from parcels of baby booties to the organization it is today. It is humbling.

Another recent adventure I had, was my first trip back to the farm where I lived for fifty-four years. Kelly, my daughter-in-law had a ramp made for my wheelchair. So when Bill's sister was visiting, Kelly invited us for a tea party. All our girls, Pat, Beth and Judy, were there and we had a wonderful time. I wondered how I would feel going back to the farm knowing Kelly had done lots of redecorating, I wondered if it would bother me. But no such luck. It did not bother me at all. My memories were secure and I was happy in my new house and my new life.

Every once in a while, I have an exciting day. A few days ago, it was my birthday, my first one at home since I was in the hospital. All my girls showed up in the afternoon and we had two huge birthday cakes and we drank pots of teas. We had a great time and enjoyed ourselves, as we do when we are all together. Then Beth told me that her daughter was playing basketball that night at the local Sportsplex and that I was going to be taken to see her. My response was that I could not go in a wheelchair. "Why not?" she asked "It is completely accessible. Of course, you're coming." So Bill, Paulo and I went. It was wonderful! It was the first time I had ever watched a whole game anywhere. When I was child, I played softball and lived it, not watched it.

So there was me, in my wheelchair enjoying the game, no matter that I did not understand a whip. I probably had the most comfortable seat in the house. That day, I also had a phone call from Ireland, one from Germany and one from Pink Mountain up on the Alaska Highway. What more could I have asked for?

Six

Getting My Groove Back

This summer I had a wonderful surprise. When we lived on our farm, there was a little country school in our area. After the school closed, the community bought it as a Community Centre where the local population held dances, card parties and many other social events. I loved that rural school and Bill and I spent many happy hours at various events there. In fact, nearly all of my book launchings were held there. But now the school was out for me as it didn't have a wheelchair ramp. In the Spring, I heard rumors they might be building one but forgot about it. Then came the night of a steak barbeque and Bill said, "We're going, Bets. They've got the ramp done." We did go and it was wonderful being back at the Three Hills Rural School, seeing my old friends, and not only was the ramp done, my dear friends had decided Marie Rosgen and I would cut the ribbon.

Since coming home, the Red Deer Hospital has built a large new thirty-bed stroke unit with my therapist, Margaret, in charge. I hear she got the job without an interview and she'll be wonderful I know.

Now that I've been home for many months, I 've devised some exercises I do in my wheelchair. I do a series of touching my toes in a half curb. At least I try to touch my toes twenty times each. I also do a series of arm exercises with my good arm. These are exercises on just one side, so I have a vision of growing gigantic muscles on that side like one half of Arnold Schwarzenegger. I am also learning to compensate for having only one hand. I use my teeth to pull the lid off my lipstick and also to tear open envelopes and so on. But I'm really looking for crafts I can do with one hand.

I had a neat experience last week. Paulo needed eleven days off but our local hospital was booked up so I had to go to the respite room in Drumheller which is about an hour long drive from home. I'm so used to our local respite room and I like it so much, I wasn't keen on going to Drumheller. but when I got there, it was great! It's quite a new facility and really laid out well. I had a room with a good view of the Badland Hill. The staff was so wonderful but the neatest part were the programs which were held every day. What a variety! About every hour from 9:00 a.m. until 3:00 p.m. you could go to a program: Mental Aerobics, Craft Time and Bingo – where I enjoyed winning a banana, some crackers and cheese, and even a tube of Avon lipstick. Yes, I know, small things amuse me.

I went to a craft session where we were to make Chia Pets using a nylon anklet stuffed with a layer of shavings then a layer of dirt and some grass seed. The idea is for the seed to grow through the nylon and your Chia Pet has a full head of green hair. As we were filling our socks, one of the patients thought the shavings were food and started eating. Another was stuffing her pockets with the soil. About then, I wondered why I was there. Most of the people on my ward were stroke victims but were also somewhat mentally deficient. I just had to chuckle at their antics and ignore it all. Once I did this, I was fine. The nurses were wonderful with them. They were always hugging, teasing and laughing with them. I was told the real mental cases were in the next ward, so again I found a reason to count myself lucky. I kept going to every class no matter how juvenile. A lot of the nurses treat the patients as children which I soon saw was the best way.

One day I saw a program coming up that caught my eye – an art class with Trev. At first I felt I wouldn't go as I'm the most unartistic person in the world, but I did go. Trev asked me what I'd like to paint and I told him, "A mountain scene."

We discussed it, he mixed the watercolors and guided me along. The painting took shape with Trev touching it up here and there. By the end of the class I had a painting that pleased me. I had done it with one hand – my wrong one at that – and one eye. My! I was smug when I gave it to Bill. The dear man said he was going to frame it. I really enjoyed painting that picture. I thought I could paint many more, go in my wheelchair and sit at some corner on a street in Calgary and sell them. I could even put a black patch on my bad eye for effect. What a hoot that would be!

The eleven days which I thought would be endless really zipped by. One day, all my girls came down, took me to Liquidation World, and what a riot that was! We managed really well getting me in and out of the car. In fact, I felt absolutely, blissfully free. Another day there was a book fair at the hospital. Oh, did I have fun with that! I bought books for everyone, then after dropping off the first load in my room, I had the nurse take me to the fair again where I bought another two full bags of books. If it was there the next day, I'd probably have gone again!

You might think I'm a little insane enjoying such small things, but in my new life I *must* and *do* have to make my life enjoyable. I'm succeeding!

Seven

Inspiration

In closing, I just want to say that it has been sixteen months since my stroke and I am still improving both in body and spirit. Things that I thought I could never live with, I have found I can. I thought I could never live with having lost partial sight in my one good eye. This worried me more than anything and bothered me terribly. I was always after the doctor to bring in a specialist and quizzed him constantly about whether my eyesight would get better. The specialist told me that it may improve slowly but that it would not get worse. Still, I was not accepting this, but I always got the same answer.

Now at this stage, after having been home for some months, whether the sight has improved or whether I have adjusted to it I can't say but I do know that I hardly notice anything at all. I have completely got over any sense of modesty whatsoever. It took me a while, but I have got used to being waited on. I do still get annoyed if people try to do things for me that I can do for myself, like feeding me. The rest is just commonplace now. I still push myself constantly to improve myself, but I am not in any panic. My right arm is still not working but I am not giving up and Paulo works on it every day. If it does not come back, I will accept that too.

I sure miss my knitting and crocheting. I have recently heard about a knitting machine which only requires the use of one arm, so I am thinking about that. I will find some other handiwork to do as well. My right leg is still not back completely. I walk every day at home with a cane. I don't let my mind dwell on what I can't do such as driving and cooking.

With Spring here, my thoughts are on the flower boxes which I love but I knew I couldn't plant them. Kelly said she would get the plants and put them in. On the day of planting she came in and said, "Come out on the deck Betty, and you can help." I can't do anything but it would be nice to be outside. But Paulo pushed me right beside the boxes where I could actually plant with my good arm. It felt so good getting my fingers in the dirt. Some of the plants looked a little crooked but it didn't matter. The neighbor started up the lawn mower and the smell of newly cut grass was wonderful. The birds were singing and it was a little touch of heaven for me, that moment in time.

My life now is very happy. My wish came true. I am back home with my beloved Bill and yes, I still put makeup on each morning and follow it with a good shot of perfume.

If you are going through what I did, keep your spirits up. Look to the positive always – there is *always* a positive, you know – and lock into it. The things you can do, enjoy; and the things you can't live with, you will find in a few months you can. You will accept the things you can't. Find humor in every event and put your hand in God's hand. He is there for you at all times.

So when you find yourself trying to roll and balance on a big beach ball or practice pivoting, or doing yet ten more pushups or walking yet *another* twenty steps and feel you can't continue and you want to just quit, remember you are climbing a mountain. You will reach the top and when you get there you'll find it gets so much easier on the way down. The view is brighter than you thought it could be, you see the light and realize you have made it.

Remember, you have more strength than you think you have. Hang in there and you can do it! I can tell you right now that I am home, happy, and there *is* life after a stroke. I promise you.

Prologue

Since writing the first draft of this book, a few things have changed.

Paulo no longer has to drive all the way to Calgary to visit Sally. They've since married and now his lovely new bride lives here with us and Paulo has some competition in the kitchen!

The group from Acme will soon be leaving on their journey and will return with stories of their own to tell. I'm looking forward to hearing them all.

Now that Summer has passed and the Fall sales are drawing to an end, I can hardly wait to see the new Sears Wish Book!

Appendix A:

❖ ❖ ❖ ❖ ❖ ❖ ❖ ❖

Progressive Short Stay Rehabilitation Program for Stroke Patients

❖ ❖ ❖ ❖ ❖ ❖ ❖ ❖

The Progressive Short Stay Rehabilitation Program operates as a four-bed unit located in the Dr. Richard Parsons Care Center at the Red Deer Regional Hospital Center. In this environment, a team of health professionals will help guide you and your family/caregiver toward your highest level of physical, emotional, and spiritual health.

The Goal: The goal of the Program is to assist you to function with as much independence as possible within your own community.

Who Qualifies? The Program is designed for individuals in the David Thompson Health Region who have recently had a stroke and would benefit from these services. You may be eligible for the Program if you:

- are 16 years of age or older;
- require more than one rehabilitation service;
- are medically stable;
- have the potential motivation, and desire to be rehabilitated to a higher level of functioning.

Referral Process: Referral by your doctor is required for you to be considered for the Program. Acceptance into the Program is based on screening done by the Assessment Team to ensure that you meet the admission standards for the unit. In the event of a waiting list, you will be accepted according to our prioritization system.

Discharge: The average length of stay is 4 – 12 weeks. Plans for discharge begin upon admission to the Program. Conferences will be held with you and your family/caregiver to discuss your treatment goals and your progress. To prepare you for discharge, you will be expected to go home on regular weekend visits with family support as required. When you have reached your goal, or would no longer benefit from the Program, you will be discharged. Appropriate community and support services will be put in place prior to discharge.

Commitment: The Program is designed with you and your family/caregiver as an essential part of the rehabilitation process. It is expected that you and your family/caregiver will participate in the treatment process, decision making, and discharge planning. Your cooperation and input are key elements to your success in the Program.

Purpose:

• To assist patients to function as independently as possible within the community, and/or to reduce their care to as minimal a level as possible.

• To reduce the length of stay for the patient in the acute care bed after the initial period of acute illness

• To decrease the chances of readmission of the patient resulting from a discharge before the patient/family were equipped to manage independently.

• To prevent discharge to a facility not able to offer levels of rehabilitation necessary for the patient to reach his/her full potential.

•To avoid unnecessary transitions that will affect the patient's progress due to adjustment to a new environment.

Appendix B

Paulo Cardano

My name is Paulo Cardano. I was born in Quezon City, Philippines, which is a few minutes drive from the capital, Manila, ignoring the heavy traffic though!

The main reason I came to Canada was to look for a better job opportunity. A job that would pay enough to support my family back home and enable me to start to save for my own future. After I had learned about the "Live-In Caregiver Program" in Canada through the Internet, I gave up my job as a Quality Controller. I then decided to enroll in a training center that trains people applying for the job of caregiver in Canada. The modules of the training included child care, elderly or senior care, care for the physically and mentally challenged, home management, Canadian history and basic French (which I did not pay too much attention to back then).

I trained for almost seven months and with the help of an agency based in Calgary, I was able to find a couple in need of a caregiver. My clients would be this couple's two young sons, ages 10 and 7-years-old. I was to look after the boys especially while their parents were out to work.

It took quite a while before I received my work visa allowing me to enter Canada to work as a caregiver. I had to wait five months before receiving my interview notice from the Canadian Embassy in Manila and a medical examination and then another two month wait until the courier arrived with my visa. They called it the "normal processing time."

I flew into Vancouver on Cathay pacific on October 29, 2002. I then flew on a connecting Air Canada flight to Calgary. My employers and their sons were there to welcome me and to pick me up. I heard the eldest son, Jojo, say "You're right on time for the first day of Winter." It was a traumatic experience for me the first time I stepped out of the warm Calgary airport into a cold winter day. The cold weather really shook me up.

It was so much fun working for them. The boys and I had lots of fun together. They considered me as their big brother even though they both spoke better English than me.

Unfortunately my stay with them did not last long due to some personal problems with the family.

Using my newly acquired electric typewriter (purchased at a garage sale), I updated my resume and made several copies. I then began answering ads from the newspapers provided courtesy of my girlfriend Sally, who by the way, I married in March 2004 (Sorry Betty, I just want to take this opportunity to tell Sally how much she really means to me. Hon, I love you so much!).

Anyway, on July 2, 2003, a day after spending my first Canada Day with Sally at Prince's Island Park, I received a phone call from Bill. He asked me if I would be willing to live outside Calgary and be the caregiver for his wife. If my memory serves me right, I think the only word I said to him at that time was "Yes!"